W0254255

TROUBLED

A memoir in poems and fragments

RM Vaughan

COACH HOUSE BOOKS | TORONTO

first edition

Canada Council for the Arts Conseil des Arts du Canada

Canada

Published with the generous assistance of the Canada Council for the Arts and the Ontario Arts Council. Coach House Books also acknowledges the Government of Canada through the Book Publishing Industry Development Program.

LIBRARY AND ARCHIVES CANADA CATALOGUING IN PUBLICATION

Vaughan, R. M. (Richard Murray), 1965–
Troubled : A memoir in poems and fragments / R. M. Vaughan.

ISBN 978-1-55245-198-4

I. Title.

PS8593.A94T76 2008 C811'.54 C2008-901388-3

For Kirsten Johnson, who got up early and held my hand.

A forgery is impossible when we have no model to forge after.
H. P. Blavatsky *Isis Unveiled*

But there is no such thing as secrecy.
Theodor Fontane *Effi Briest*

It is not a matter of words for things. Rather it is a matter of distance between the word and the thing.
Nathalie Stephens *Touch to Affliction*

SESSION

Orchids, a man who breeds orchids   (Faulkner's pet hate,
their hoary throats and stick-insect limbs   unnerving harbingers,
Nasty things he wrote, in bed, tingly with bursitis and drink.
Their flesh is too much like the flesh of men,
and their perfume has the rotten sweetness of corruption)   if only that.

So, he parents orchids, my latest psychiatrist,
and watercolours, by the metre   so many beach fronts,
fir groves, rose gold maples, whirling brooks and blotch flowers.
An outdoorsman, hobby artist   unoriginal but energetic
(already, my critic voice, already   five minutes past the office door)
and so, too, his body   a recap
of all the top muscle groups of the nineties – the baseball bicep,
the cleft chest, shoulders like whale backs and a teen waist
tucked into purple and yellow plaid –
Easter colours in September (*stop it stop it stop it*).

Because he knows my type, my talents, he begins with rules
(we critics love rules, and are all bottoms):   I must not be late, not cancel,
not lie, expect, begrudge, sour, shirk,
disrespect the process, steal the magazines, pick the flowers,
wear muddy shoes, treat him like a friend.

SESSION

On a flowered couch, I seed   crack like milkweed pods
in frost, spores in mud
        call all the old gods to harvest.
                                        My father, mad as a paper kettle,
as three glass balls in a blender.   My mother, her sleepy violence,
a limbless she-cat, all caterwaul and cant.
        My body, a wrung pillow
and the quiet habits of rough sex, for spice.

He flexes, winds his fingers.   Takes no notes, no notice.

All my embarrassments, summoned, cast on the floor –
runes and bones and shiny stones – our first magic, first sniff
of the glands, presenting of horns.   And he says, only,
Save something for later.

SESSION

Good material, he snicks (because I write, my stolen baby nights,
bedtimes robbed by Dad – who knocked on walls, the ghost tapper,
and cried over westerns, *Roots* and two wars he never fought,
played magus with paper pyramids, telescopes trained
to Martian highways, feared white sugar –
are now metaphor, *only metaphor* games of match
and mend to the doctor). *Good material*, he grins.

Not sores, not slits, not lead in my blood.
Not turned limbs set with pipe cleaners, not scabs,
heart spurs, ticks, kinks, the way I walk but blessings
full of iron and plot twists burnt sweets, these memories,
strong black coal for the censer and …

The best possible start, he smiles,

shaking my hand and his head at the door.

SESSION

In his waiting room, wet jasmine in goldfish pots
white as Christmas   and five new paintings
– a fat frog on a reed mat   a birch stand pencilled with flame
slush and rocks   waves and rocks   lawns and rocks –
then, two blonde women, local Greeks in rayon,
worried by phantom gripe, spectral scratches   same as me …

He waves me in, grins backwards at the cheap Helens,
an ape baring incisors, red gums.

We're comrades   four shoulders, two cocks,
men who flinch and wink at arias,
the woman's cult of tea and torment,
at shakes, nerves, jags, mists, humours and fancies.

Because no man has marked me a man, ever,
I could just cry.

SESSION

Behind a burgundy Blood Leaf, pruned for spring
to spokes, red wands   beneath an Inuit stone raccoon   (do raccoons skitter
so far north, turn white like tundra hares?)   he finds
The Seven Habits of Highly Effective People
slaps the back cover on his thigh   a pitcher summoning patience,
suggests I catch.

I take the challenge home, smarting   the pages smell of old coffee,
the underneaths of beds,
of highly ineffective patients not habituated to literature.

Page 71, four dried leaves (oak, pinched in green bloom)
plus a Saint Cecilia bookmark smudged with cardamom, banded in blue felt

Page 133, evidence of a sneeze

Page 259, in pencil, under the fourth paragraph   *God Alone*,
then, three ochre sketches of lions sporting crayon crowns
and smouldering spears

Page 282, all commas reamed to fibre with a blunt pin
perhaps a barrette clasp or unwound spring   a watch hand, an apple stem,
whatever you use when knives and visits are not allowed

Page 304, a sticker, nickel sized (black kittens riding jack o' lanterns)
and a warning, underlined with dabs of cooking oil, the spent end of a match,
spit and eyelashes
he will liy so you now but be OK? he liys like a bastard dog
like all the carpets in the castle
he's a smart watcher so watch back!   be Ok

SESSION

Nervous sorts, my fellow patients: the man with hair like watered felt
picking his hands   the woman who stomps   the boy in black lipstick
with half a left ear   three seniors,
brother sister brother, ugly and alike, pill hounds,
and David, my old friend David.

We have agreed to say nothing by saying nothing   but he is always early
and nearly teary.
So what is there to say?

SESSION

Because Doctor collects, today we chat about collections:
rare guppy breeds, ugly wine labels from Germany (gnomes, stags,
chastised children, endless chubby monks), gold stocks,
Doris McCarthy landscapes (winters only), holiday socks   all his.
Then, my habit of hoarding calendula seeds, cat whiskers and found cassettes,
Chinese deities I can't identify.   He takes a note, whistles.

I had a patient once, a man. Collected bridges. Bridge spotter.
But he wouldn't cross one, not even a plank across a puddle,
until I cured him, took him for a slow walk over the Bloor viaduct,
held his hand like a baby.
Now he's into chamber music. Berlioz and Bach, Gregorian chants,
constant Classical 96. Even went to Venice.

A Buddhist proverb I remember too late:
If the Buddha leads you to a far peak
kill him at the top.

SESSION

He's been reading my books (my stupid fault,
boasting of shortcuts to me of scrub trails in type,
limp pats of grass, meadow lanes between the bindings,

of hunting lines, hound wakes and cat paths in ink
visible only to psychotics and doctors of transparencies,
tamped-down patches in the lustrous glades of rag cloth
and lies).

So now he's excited, he's found a blue vein.
It's all so CBC, so reverent and hushed.
He invests my poems with reverb and boom.

I am flattered as a kiss-polished baby
to be read so close.

SESSION

Three dreams, two dismissals (mine, his)   a lovers' breakfast idyll
without toast   first light, jam jars, sleep crusts or foggy kisses
without the lovers.

A man chases me, the Golem in dress slacks, a mud man,
iron pikes for fingers   no shoes and clumped toes,
the streets race to fields to red deserts to small rooms,
vases break, of course   and all my dead pets call my name.

Under a torched tree, I make bracelets and belts
from crisped bark   happy as a dry toddler.

The desert, again   something with Masai hunters and whips,
an S/M pastoral:
unimaginable cocks, red asses (and more dead pets),
my body lean as iris shoots   flush with sex.

You're just horny,
(well yes you idiot yes
here I am right now   it is midsummer inside me)
and underemployed
(like all pets)

but very entertaining.

SESSION

Like all lean men, Doctor mistrusts fatties,
us buffet lollers and cheesecake cowards,
thinks me palsied, short-breathed   faint before hills and bicycles.

In my fantasies I am surprisingly calm on rollerblades,
he directs me down silvery canals,
past low lichen wastes pocked with flowers-of-sage,
over turtle beds and railway ties,
pop-cup mounds and raccoon nests,
sunless undersides of bridges best for kisses.

We slink and hurtle, take corners like ice cream licks,
stop to fresh our tongues with pineapple mint,
Bengal almond fudge, clear spit,
wrestle and tussle and rise uncertain,
brakes at heels   then aim, thighs tempered
for the low, cold lake,
waving at dogs and senile widows,
lone men haunting the high musky grass,
the chokecherry hamams,
at anyone in love.

Half awake, I am athletic and sleek   fat only
if porpoises are thought fat, if otters too
or full afternoons, hovering jets, ripe berries   fat as a bullet.

Look at me, S——, look at me   cognitive therapy doesn't work
on romantics.

'The Canadian Medical Association's code of ethics states succinctly: "A physician ... will scrupulously avoid using the physician–patient relationship to gratify his own emotional, ... financial and sexual needs" (Canadian Psychiatric Association, 2002).

'Boundary violations occupy a spectrum of behaviours that range in terms of frequency and harmfulness. Some authors make a distinction between boundary violations (which cause harm) and boundary crossings (which do not) (Gutheil & Gabbard, 1993). The problem with this distinction is that boundary crossings may be repeated and may develop into boundary-violating behaviours over time; also, it is not clear who will decide whether a behaviour might or has caused harm.'[1]

SESSION

Kitten stupid, I take the bait   unwind all the Murray Stories
the misadventures of my bughouse dad,
he who made me what I am.

Story Nine – The War Years:

Mother, rattled and cold, stunned inside
from decades of separate beds, apart minds,
drives Murray to a country analyst   the berry-farm Freud
experienced in all husbandries, electrical cures,
a believer in plain talk, insulin shock, distracting hobbies,
breath control   nerve pills, bath salts   *exercise*
that last resort of unimaginative shrinks.

Murray entertains, all fiddles and spoons,
sweats horrors ripped from *Sgt. Rock* – Japanese camps
and Indonesian alligators, the cruelties of jungles   of bamboo
clinking on bone and swamp frenzies   insects
dexterous with needles   how to kill a man
with two thumbs and a matchstick …

The rustic Jung, seduced by blood, bounces to my mother,
notes and case studies and healing books at his elbow,
numbers and names at Veteran's Affairs.

But Murray wasn't in the war   Mother snaps,
worn and unsurprised.

My doctor claps his desk, rises to wire a carmine orchid
tight as a saddle strap:

My father was Scottish,
he never told a story in his life.

SESSION

So far, similes   palmed coins, shirks, two-steps
in lieu of marches, little shuffles
on hot coals, in army boots   feint work, goldbrick skips.

Pol Pot: 'A metaphor is a singing lie.'

Enough tugs and coverlets, hand jive.   I love him and comparison
is odious.

SESSION

I am troubled by how I live – in rooms wiped with lime utility paint,
in houses dirty as telephone poles, with bay leaves for moth bane,
glue and paper curtains, with single women who pant
like generators for their boyfriends and don't read.
Always under someone's stairs: a goblin, a fat sprite,
ugly as a bent gate but less effective.

Look at me and say   *No, no, Richard, I would not fool with the devil*
for a clean bed, orchids at table and almond-oil rubs,
his moneyed hands on my ass.

FROM MY SPELL DIARY   APRIL 16, 1998

A blue pen and ragged cap, for the impression of his teeth,
dipped in new sweet wine   a brown switch of goldfish weed
because he pet-names his plants   bound in white thread
for constancy   coins from the client couch
thrown three times onto red silk   copper constellations.

A tin Eiffel tower from his desk, hung with electrical wire
above a live wick. One prescription note, shoved
down the front of my pants and rubbed
to sweet pulp inside my legs – the lowest of charms.

Thumbprint, left, from sticky cover of *Maclean's* (hopefully his)
cut five times, ridge to centre   then boiled for tea
(the 'Roman cure,' last hope of fading virgins and fatties).

Nineteen paperclips, straightened to shivs, silver minnows,
nine for each shoe, and one to cut with.

HARLEQUIN ROMANCE TITLES

The Doctor's Secret Child
The Italian Doctor's Mistress
The Good Doctor
The Celebrity Doctor's Proposal
The Flight Doctor's Lifeline
The Doctor's Special Touch
The Doctor's Fire Rescue
The Doctor's Latin Lover
The Doctor's Rescue Mission
The Doctor's Pregnancy Surprise
The Baby Doctor's Desire
The Police Doctor's Secret
The Doctor's Tender Secret
Emergency: Bachelor Doctor!

PORN TITLES

The Doctor, the Lawyer and the Indian Chief
Cock Doctor
The Doctor Will Screw You Now
Head Doctor
Let's Play Doctor
The Doctor's Visit
Doctor D. P.
Doctor Spank
Doctor Knot
Doctor Discipline
The Deviant Doctor
The Doctor Is In And Out
Medic Men
College Boy Physicals 1 & 2

EASTER THURSDAY

A tide of bran flakes and wet toast,
mulched, acidic, thrown from my diaphragm,
the lower pelvic coils   a backward
morning song sung in baby food, tea-orange tremolos.
It rings, filths the undercasing of the toilet, the part I never clean,
and circles my downed face,
a back-cast, satanic halo, muck gloriole.

Because I am always on a diet and I never diet,
because he will notice the missing ounces,
one spoonful for every inch between us.

SESSION

On a bicycle to him, left foot over pavement,
right pedal snagged   on winded Tamil newspapers
from Parliament Street (and farther), I catch
a crust of curb, a sawtooth of crushed black stones, and peel a thigh,
a forearm, whole bolts of back fat down
to where the blood waits, and deeper.

He brings me hot water in a mug, a fist of paper towels,
fatherly cautions and *buck ups* –
A helmet, Richard   does not touch me
an orange light, rubber knee pads is not pleased
to touch me   *more protection.*

We break at half session, after not-careful talk
of Canadian movies and pastel vs. oil stick, ink vs. gouache,
of Montreal rents, boulevards and castor bean leaves,
bulbs and cuttings and root balls,
of paperweights, Italy,
all our tepid governments, the spoiled Quebecois.
Of remembered burns, remembered cuts,
appendix operations and chicken pox,
of vaccine scars, his ex-wife, of first-date nerves.

SESSION

To tell it is impossible – a sea crossing on a cardboard tray,
a hike over Nepal in glass shoes.   I try, speak in damp gusts,
verb spirals   in footnotes full
as Christmas trees, bottom trawls and gillnets,
with mud in my teeth.

To tell love, name attraction …
catching bats with envelopes.

SESSION

Here is where you cut my heart,
inserted snakes in the folds, blood holes – garters
not pythons, not eels   nothing monstrous or broad,
fanged nor rattle-tipped – finger curls, not fists,
because you are so very clever, smart as salt.

You said, *We'll have to find*   *We can fix*   *We'll talk this*
and I nodded, bobbed, wet faced, a drowning man.

You said, *There are ways around.*

One gesture from disaster, isn't everything always
– the rail jump, the iced wing, the downed plate,
the slit the bruise the scald – preventable?

Here is where you said *Relax*
and meant *Come to my house, take dinner, meet my children,*
buy me a book, sit in my lap,
grow used to the hiss inside.

LAST SESSION

John's Italian Café is darker than your office   and Baldwin Street
is morbid. No one will look for me here, among the batiks
and mud prints, sandalwood earrings and Indonesian crafts,
Mother's Day restaurants famous for cheesecake
and Barbara Klunder prints   what's left of the eighties.

Of course we touch, palms to forearms   knot the linens.

And you are handsome   bullish in the shoulders, box-jawed,
tough below the trunk.

You drive like a boy, one hand to the music,
indifferent to signs   as am I, this once.

Because he was beneath our lovers' notice,
that rag-and-bottle man   a local indigent,
dirty as week-old snow   you missed him by a shoe length,
an exhalation   the beat between lips and a curse.

But how he howled, our rubbish banshee,
witches would cringe, know the omens.

I didn't look back,
check for blood, blue lights,
crows in circles or squalls of flies.

'Female physicians were more likely than the men to agree that all suspected cases of sexual impropriety committed by other physicians should be reported (58.7% vs. 50.0%), whereas the men were more likely to disagree (27.9% vs. 15.5%). The women were also more likely than the men to agree that physicians should lose their licence permanently if they were found guilty of sexual violation (62.2% vs. 43.5%), whereas the men were more likely to disagree (36.3% vs. 18.4%). Almost half of the men (46.5%) but only 28 women (14.1%) reported that concerns about accusations of sexual abuse were of importance in their clinical decisions.'[2]

No tide moves without the moon, and so
we beat the waves with bobbers and sinkers, metal fish
painted in racing-car colours, with mansions inside hulls,
pushy turbines, rubber feet and planed oars,
wood and shellac, aerated foam quilts.

Because the moon is too big to bother

we peck when we might roar.

'Based on the description of the offense and the nature of the professional relationship with the victim, offenders may be further classified into the following useful typology: incidental, interpersonal, narcissistic, exploitive, angry and sadistic types …

'Incidental offenders refer to those who have impulsively behaved in a sexually inappropriate manner and there is only one known occurrence of the behaviour. Interpersonal offenders include professionals who are motivated to establish a close, intimate and long-lasting relationship. The investment in the relationship seems genuine, without clear signs of exploitation or abuse. Narcissistic offenders include professionals who may or may not be seeking a close, emotional relationship. However, their behaviour more strongly suggests strong needs for attachment, admiration, approval, validation, love and attention. Compensatory types include professionals who are more opportunistic and impulsive, and who basically offend to fulfill unmet needs for physical closeness, affection and sexual relations. Exploitive offenders include professionals who purposely use their position of authority and power to achieve their behaviour and fulfill their needs (e.g., control, power, domination). Anger types include those who persistently sexually harass and offend … As per the nature of their behaviour, these individuals evidence strong feelings of hostility, rage and resentment … Finally, sadistic offenders correspond to those who enjoy using their power and authority to control and dominate the victim, with marked pleasure out of being cruel and provoking sufferance.

'Based on the evaluation and treatment progress, reintegration of the offender into their professional practice may or may not be recommended …'[3]

Yes, let's be equivocal, differentiate   publish and gather
our cock hairs while we may   you fuckers and best friends
of same.

Let's tune, pluck,
stare at a burning house and see
one thousand wicks winking, mesmeric flickers,
not the blaze, the char, the whole crashing mess.

It's only my heart, my heart held over
a tall, splintered pike ... all my weight pressed
on the rude point.

Just my heart, a broken ball, a pink toad
open and wet, fellow to no useful typology.

SWORD STREET

1

Your daughter is lovely and angry,
she is seventeen, a scowling barge, typical.

And you wrestle with her, still,
pin, leg lock, Indian Burn and Purple Nurple,
bunny punch and toss her   over and down, face to carpet.
Yes, it is sexual. Yes, I want some too.

She has a lot of aggression that needs to be played out.

There is always pathology in roughhousing (I should know),
always a needle in the pillow, razors in the water balloon.

My turn comes, no contest,
you burrow and spank, run duvet sorties   all thunder,
then two bolts done.
But I'm new around here.

2

You have lived too long alone to bear me, swallow so fast
hasty toast, dry-dunked in coffee.
Because I talk when I wake, no kisses at the door.

I'm already lonely and only sex shuts my mouth
(the wife under the storm drain, widow of the breakfast nook,
I write sweet half-poems in pink ink   retarded by thanks
and wonder).

This can't last, can't …

Fearsome in bed makes cozy at table
is a fable, a spinster caution

more true in reverse.

3

Blame your pills, like a good shrink.
Blame your sly chemical medley, that careful expensive syncopation
of blunters and exhilarants, quiet and hullabaloo,
liqueur and uppers,
for your unmanning.

Because it can't be me, not yet
I suppose, standing by your bed, puffy and half-socked,
unsure of my feet.   *Not yet.*

Let's sit apart, at bed ends,
undressed, innocent as flannel   and tell stories.
You know mine by heart.

NEW YORK WEEKEND

1

Level with the first haze, the 6 a.m. brown flue,
he studies his bonds, gold listings, palm-oil stocks,
the price of white pears in China   nods or
whistles   wasting the window seat
(there is good reading in money).

I tap the mineral holdings, forest leverages
and the morning rates for the skins
of minks   wet my thumb and poke the tent of numbers,
break his trail of earnings and loss.

I'm excitable, for a writer   ignoble and keen,
too happy for Air Canada,
the jet line of prairie traders and colicky Quebecois,
favoured carrier of bereaved city children inbound
for country funerals, Maritimers impatient with trains,
all us quiet northern sorts.

So I deserved his almost playful slap
(a backhand with kick, a flick,
something between a pat and a reprimand),
a pinch and a threat.

2

He entered me on MacDougal Street
(who has not wanted to write that line?)   a starling's
quarrel from Washington Square.

It was hardly Jamesian   not baroque, syntactical,
not a meandering Castle Walk or One-Step,
a ballroom of sweet bites mashed, necks pressed to thighs,
bumping, unshaved bon mots.   Not Bridge or Hearts,
anything calculated   only cock, plain cock,
fussed between low circles of muscle, then jiggered   shook out.

He slept, mocked by pigeons,
beasts that dance for their lovers.

3

There is nothing new to say about the Empire State Building,
we discover
too soon after our souvenir kiss.

4

At the Pearson Park 'n' Fly, you run to ground.

Because all Toronto faces south, to the ancient lake,
a containment pond, a tanner's pit oiled
with shit, brick scraps, misplaced pets,
moss carp fattened on balti, dog roses and pad Thai,
on generations of renewal, dream tailings …
coming home reminds us of endings.

You break my heart like you drive:
inattentive to dark corners, in spasms, ignorant
of gradations, niceties of shoulder and road,
the biting gravel at the edge of planed words.

DUFFERIN GROVE PARK

Under a tree is as good as a hotel room, library,
Versailles or truck stop   to finish an affair.

Leaves will cup to catch your threats, excuses,
twigs too thin for martins
can carry your poor lies, breaths of scandal.

On a round bench we face out, eyes to front
to clumps of waning yarrow, municipal clover,
coneflower chilled to grey spikes.

On a round bench girdling a dull, broken oak
desperate for snow, for minerals and water,
we become insupportable.

On this beaten picnic platform,
this nail-and-plank lovers' couch, a teenage perch
common as a chair, a knife, you make luxurious demands,
ask me not to speak of us, of our time.

I promise to only circumvent, or write poetry,
the second-best silence.

'Despite condemnation by ethical codes, published guidelines and policies for all the helping professions, sexual exploitation by health and mental health professionals remains a prevalent but poorly understood problem. It is estimated that half of all mental health clinicians will evaluate and/or treat at least one person who was sexually exploited by a previous psychotherapist, physician, psychiatrist or other health or helping professional.'[4]

All that comes of talking is rotation   talk is a gyro
fixed to a clock   a ticker, set tooth and groove,
in gummy sync to flywheels, tumblers,
all manner of gigs and spinnakers and greased spokes
bundled in oiled elastics,
false starts, MacGuffins, long herrings redder than pipe embers
and just as lasting.

I talked, blew on pinwheels.

Lady detectives were called, notes were sticky-tabbed.

Blue flags for our 'chance meetings' (the blinking generosity
of medical detectives, bloused badgers trained to scent
the lie of coincidence, amazes   breaks your heart).

Yellow pennants for the detailed fuckings
we planned in advance.
Pink ensigns for the performance
of said (yes, pink, dusty rose   shit-blush).

When she instructed   *describe his penis*   a fat pen
rolling under her palm   without irony

I said   *not long, but pointed.*

Listen, Doc, here's a piece of advice. Never say 'I Love You' when you're horny. The words don't count. It's like buying groceries before dinner – you forget what you need. People have to learn to manage their needs. You taught me that.

So now, it's out. I Love You. Everything is different.

You hear that whistling sound? It's the bullet. You can't take the bullet back.

Guns are very specific tools. You can pull an arrow out of a heart and use it again. You can flush poison down the toilet. You can wipe off the candlestick in the kitchen or hide the lead pipe in the library. But a gun makes an awful mess.

Even the bullets that miss make a hole in the wall. The shells won't fit back in the chamber and the powder burns your hands. No two bullets are alike. Liars always leave a trail. But lying to a liar is just plain stupid.[5]

FOUR THINGS I DID INSTEAD OF KILLING YOU

Covered my head in borage petals, flushes of scald (bleach,
lemon juice and flat Stetson), slept off the burn.

Imagined I had no shame.

Made art as ineffective as a sheepdog
in a twister, yapping down the funnel, fur flat,
ears over my nape, tail between tits.

Told, told on you. Gentlemen's veils
be damned.

R.M. Vaughan
807 College St.
#304
Toronto, ON
M6G 1C9

February 5, 1999

Re: Response to Dr. █████'s statement, dated January 27/99.
HC/comment/40826

Dear Ms. Carroll,

I have read over Dr. █████'s statement and have the following comments.

The first three paragraphs, in which Dr. █████ describes his qualifications and the history of my therapy with him are, to my knowledge, accurate.

The fourth paragraph, however, contains many innacuracies and ommissions.

Firstly, Dr. █████ describes meeting me "unexpectedly" at a theatre festival. This is not true.

Dr. █████ specifically attended the opening night performance of a play written by me, entitled The Susan Smith Tapes. Dr. █████ and I discussed this play during therapy, and he expressed interest in seeing the production. Our meeting was far from "unexpected", as he told me in therapy that he intended to see the play.

I will not speculate as to why Dr. █████ wishes to portray our first non-therapeutic meeting as accidental.

Secondly, I find the term used by Dr. █████, "emotional relationship", confusing and vague. It appears to me that Dr. █████ is attempting to deny or obscure the sexual nature of our relationship.

Thirdly, Dr. █████'s description of his depression is an accurate, but not full account. While Dr. █████ was under "psychiatric treatment" during our sexual relationship, this treatment, to my knowledge, was administered by a doctor in British Columbia, whom Dr. █████ saw very infrequently.

Furthermore, Dr. █████ continued to work full time during this period. While I do not question that Dr. █████ was indeed depressed, this fact strikes me as both a "red herring" in regards to his conduct with me, and, ultimately irrelevant in how his conduct should be judged.

Fourthly, his statement that I was "aware of these circumstances" is, to be blunt, infuriating to me. My awareness of Dr. █████'s depression has nothing to do with the fact that we entered into an inappropriate sexual relationship. Dr. █████ appears to be implying that my knowledge of his depression somehow lessens the exclusivity of his culpability. Dr. █████ is employing a "blame the victim" strategy in his defense.

Finally, Dr. █████'s offer of a mediated meeting strikes me as insincere and merely a formality. I attempted to meet with Dr.

[redacted] several times following the end of our sexual relationship, and he consistently avoided personal contact with me - resorting instead to occasional phone messages of little substance. I see no benefit in such a meeting now.

In conclusion, my assesment of Dr. [redacted]'s statement is that Dr. [redacted] is attempting to dodge the issue of our sexual relationship by admitting, in part, to everything else.

After reading Dr. [redacted]'s letter, I am afraid that my complaint against him may be reduced to a case of two conflicting accounts - and, personally, I wonder how inclined the College is to take the word of a patient over a fellow doctor? Dr. [redacted] appears to be positioning himself to benefit from the favourable bias of his colleagues.

Because of my above concern, I feel compelled to remind your investigation of the many witnesses I have listed who can recall seeing Dr. [redacted] and myself in situations of a romantic and/or sexual nature; including his two daughters.

Thank you for your providing me with Dr. [redacted]'s statement.

Sincerely,

R.M. Vaughan

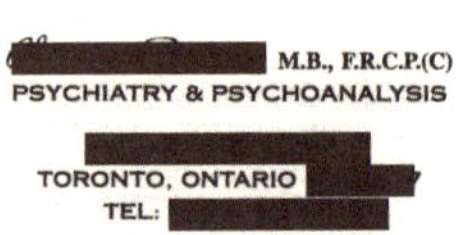

6th July 1999

PRIVATE AND CONFIDENTIAL

Ms.
Investigations & Resolutions,
The College of Physicians and Surgeons of Ontario,
80 College St.,
Toronto, ON M5G 2E2

Dear Ms. ,

Re: Mr. Richard Vaughan

Mr. Vaughan first came to see me on the 8th June 1998. He was interested in short-term psychotherapy to help him deal with his distress at the ending of his affair with his former psychiatrist.

He was aware, before he came to me, that should he reveal the name of the psychiatrist, I would have to report to the College. He decided that he wanted to sort out his feelings about the relationship before he gave me the name.

On the 20th July 1998 Mr. Vaughan told me that Dr. was the psychiatrist with whom he had been sexually involved.

At our first meeting Mr. Vaughan appeared anxious and distressed. He reported that he had been seeing Dr. in psychotherapy for a two year period. He found him helpful and supportive and felt that things were moving along. In early February 1998 he told Dr. that he was very attracted to him. Mr. Vaughan thought this was transference and was surprised and overjoyed when Dr. said that he reciprocated the feelings. Mr. Vaughan said that Dr. started to show up in his social world. Within a week they were sexually involved and the psychotherapy was terminated.

The affair lasted approximately eight weeks. Mr. Vaughan said his feelings were very intense and he wanted to make the relationship work. When Dr. abruptly ended it. Mr. Vaughan was very upset and confused. The implications of having this affair and the sudden ending were profound. I quote "If this person who knew me best of anyone on the planet loved me and then stopped who will love me".

Course in Therapy

During the first six weeks Mr. Vaughan agonized over whether to report Dr. ████ He felt intense shame about the affair and did not want to be seen as a victim. This alternated with a desire to prevent Dr. ████ from causing the same distress to another patient.

Mr. Vaughan struggles with trust, he is aware o his need for an intense emotional attachment but, is wary of the motives of others. He quickly shies away from potentially intimate connections, fearing he will be trapped or that he will cause pain to others. He has had panic attacks when performing at work, and socially, afraid that he will be seen as disappointing.

I have been impressed with Mr. Vaughan's candor in discussing this relationship. He has demonstrated insight into his own difficulties and an ability to reflect on his own motives.

I hope this report answers your questions.

Yours truly,

████ M.B.,F.R.C.P.(C)

THREE HUMILIATIONS, WITH OUTBURSTS

Welts on my shoulders, impossible to cover
with thin YMCA towels, linens bleached back
to tissue.
Nobody believes 'bike accident,' 'fell on the ice,'
or 'rare vein disease,'
and 'I hate myself, hate myself, hate myself,
I rake my back
with chickweed stalks and Tiger Balm' is a hell
of a mouthful.

When the heart stops, resort to nerve –
anything that will still jump and not remember why.

The North Toronto boyfriend of a sister of a friend,
so many removes,
English-educated, heir to an orthopaedics fortune,
is unsupportive (and misses the irony).
You knew this would happen.

The privileged are never vulnerable
to complexities, to rhythms more symphonic
than the clomp-clomp of high-saddle sense.

There are exactly eight sensible books
on patient-doctor panky in the filmy carrels
and spore wells of the Toronto Public Library.
Eight books, by eight doctors.

If only I'd been fucked by a Kennedy,
an alien, Mick Jagger or Louis XVI.

I think it's okay to hurt people sometimes, even maliciously, because at least the other person can hate you for it and then life sort of settles into place by itself – everybody has a part to play. But if you go around disappointing people, you're really cruel.

When you disappointed me, you took away my power to be angry – because I still love you, I still believe in you, I just wish you'd change. When you disappointed me, it was like you came to my house and poured poison on my floor. Suddenly, poison was in the air, on my clothes, in my food, even in my hair. The poison crept into my secret, secret corners – and pretty soon it didn't really matter who made the mess in the first place.[6]

Wrong again.

Poison thins, gets pissed away,
finds a wrinkle, a flap of fat, and rests, patient
as a polyp.

He resists all scalpels – three boyfriends, the blessing
of my father's death, local fame and sex with nobodies
in a Florida basement,
lunch at the Pyramids, lunch at the Tate,
flower tea and seed cake in Antwerp,
a foundling cat to love, sunbaths and steam rooms,
menthol on my temples, novelty
and comfort.

Nothing cuts him out, disabuses me,
because he made the mess,
first place and now.

80 COLLEGE STREET, TORONTO, CANADA M5G 2E2

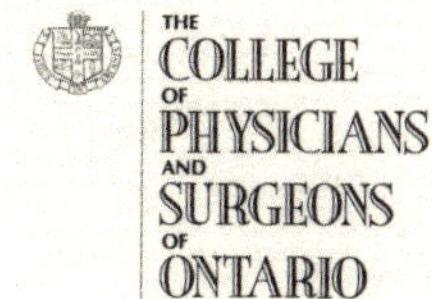

FAX: (416) 961-3330
TOLL FREE: (800) 268-7096
TEL: (416) 967-2600

IN REPLY PLEASE QUOTE: HC/

RECEIVED FROM: Mr. Richard Vaughan.

THE FOLLOWING ITEM(S):

#1 Photo - Dr. ███
#2 " " " + Mr. Vaughan
#3 Card not dated.
#3A Envelope
#4. Key to 10 Sword St.
#5 Card.
#6 Letter from Dr. ███
#7 Book
#8 Letter from Dr. ███.
#9 Card. - Dated Feb '98
#10 Jewellery chain.

[signature]
Witness

Dec 1/98
Date

Dec 1/98
Date

#11 "Playbill" Book
Gross Indecency

#12 "Playbill" Book
Bees in Honey Drown

#13 Brochure - Empire
State Building

#14 Art Now Gallery Guide
Mar 98

#15 Sketch of ███ apartment #10 ███ St. Toronto.

Protecting the public . . . guiding the profession

FIVE SMALL THINGS I KEPT FROM THE DETECTIVE

One orchid seed, dirty cobalt, spore-spattered,
ripe with poison   pinched from your favourite specimen, baby,
your precious   just in case.

Half a Walkman headphone, left ear speaker,
abandoned under your bed   a castle for mites,
brave tasters of your blood.

Two plum-infused votives
you refused to burn   presents from a lady client.
I will have my small revenges.

A dead guppy, its stomach chewed back
to the spine   what pretty little cannibals you keep.
It dried so neatly, a garnet brooch.

A poem, 'richards kises' (double sic), in rhyme,
for pity's sake.

THE HEARING

July 28, 2000, 80 College Street

9 a.m.

Such attractive lawyers' work, this dismantling of a man –
lancet skirts, bull-nose pumps, blouses in shovel colours.

And you sit there, the man, stupid and muscular   immune
to glamour, mine or yours.
It's like watching adders swallow cold eggs,
a grass fire blanketing a dry mound, spurs
cutting mud.

Like you didn't know this day was coming.

2 p.m.

I'm a spectre here, a film, gauze and netting,
the gummy skin under the rim of the cauldron.
Nothing to notice, attend. Told to stay quiet,
make no sighs, whistles, wolf calls or raspberries
during *my* day, *my* docket debut.

The irony of calling this expert busywork, this trading
of parboiled truths and medicated guesses,
this barter of lies for conclusions,
these mending feints,
a 'hearing'
escapes me, the unheard.

But I watch you, dare to
practice my phantom testimonies
the way mutes dream of replicating birdsong –
lips together, teeth ajar.

A BREAK IN THE PROCEEDINGS

I once wrote
'I could believe in Love if I didn't fall into it
every day.'

All my poems double back, perform cross-curses,
maledictions in meter, and cleverness is twice that,
is vanity reflux   I had it coming

Because I do Love you, careless and evil man,
and I do fall, every day, and it is not balletic, not feline,
it is belly first, arms wreathing head
in disbelief, cascades of neck fat, butter ripples
and foot bottoms ass up, pink as slapped foreheads,
a clown show, this Love, with full cannon
confetti and pop guns.

Because I do Love you

still, somewhere in the hottest parlour
of this house – your house, I've torched
beam to basement – sits a candelabra
gay as a poppy, drizzled in crystal
with seven unmarred birthday candles,
one for every week you gave, and took.

Dr. S—— M—— M——

Toronto

ALLEGATION

It is alleged that Dr. M—— is guilty of sexual abuse. In 1998, Dr. M—— engaged in a five-week sexual relationship with a patient, shortly after ending the professional relationship.

PLEA

Guilty

DECISION

Guilty

PENALTY

The Committee makes the following Order as to penalty:

1. The certificate of registration of Dr. S—— M—— M—— is hereby revoked.

2. Dr. M—— is directed to appear before the panel to be reprimanded.

3. Dr. M—— is required to reimburse the College for funding provided for his patient under the program required under Section 85.7 of the Health Professions Procedural Code.

Dr. M—— waived his right of appeal and the reprimand was administered.

To get over you, two more of you:
an Irish Behaviourist sex phobic, frocks by Duran Duran,
novelty bisques, chenille bears and a basement office on St. Clair –
all wheat palettes and no details (decorative nor spoken).

Then, Dr. C——, nice as milk,
at least his toy poodle had teeth.

Still, I dream of messy kills, guttings,
stunts careless of bones, fatty hide, piss and bile,
the woody cords of necks.
Do you dream me, S——?
Am I green as the grave in your arms?

I had a nervous breakdown. I was scared of everything. I was scared of tap water, scared of my plants, my CDs, *the telephone, my furniture, my books, the colour of my walls. It was not very glamorous. Most people go nuts and decide that the* CIA *is after them, that their dead relatives are watching, or that Tom Cruise is sending them frightening messages through* Entertainment Tonight. *I guess I don't aim very high. Forget Tom Cruise or the* CIA, *I was scared of my pillows.*

Pretty soon, I was just scared of being scared. If I thought something might scare me, I avoided it – say, for instance, the fridge door. But if I avoided the fridge door, I became scared that I was going to starve. When I became scared that I was going to starve, I became scared of my shoes, because you have to put on your shoes to go down the street to the grocery store, because if you don't have groceries, you starve. Get it?[7]

A curse, wrapped in the polka dot
paper of art, the prettiest sort of nonsense,
nothing to fear, abide by, confront
as dangerous, as alarming as blown-glass
swizzle sticks, miniature balsa furniture, rice
paper shadow puppets. If I had a trade
– pipe fitting, boiler making, accountancy –
I'd make you pay.

And now, this new idiot's revenge,
all slurs and wobbles, dainty stings,
poetry, for pity's sake … a broken knife
outmoded as telegrams, protest
postcards to Burmese generals, tide-kicking
sun worship, hoodoo, Methodism,
silent movies, menorahs in June, my career,
horseshoe charms and flocked paper,
the practice, performance and very idea
of regret.

Find this trinket and repent,
call, send a fruit basket,
a spray of apologies in ferns and violets
spell out *I'm Sorry* in flower language,
pant husky, wet sonnets. Fix me.

WILD ABANDON

Sex is a distraction, stupid sex a deliverance.

What inspired carnality you bred, what backroom,
blacked-out, knees-on-cement, tongue-to-boots, ass-akimbo
hilarities, what fevers of footsy   a patty-cake pyrexia,
tearless and joyless, renewed nightly.

I wanted you and I wanted you fucked out of me
and the world is full of helpful men.
I fed the cold, I fed the fever.

You, I hear, went to British Columbia.
I win again.

CODA
2005

'At last I'd have a change of role: no longer would I be the prey tracked down by a relentless hunter, I'd be the deep familiar forest ... No longer would I stagger from disaster to disaster, from one lacerating nightmare to another; I'd be the sunlit clearing and the stream. And it seemed to me that this final adventure would be even more dangerous than the others, because, for once, I couldn't imagine how it would end.'[8]

... Dr. M— is a skilled manipulator of people, especially the vulnerable. I should know, as I was deeply and profoundly manipulated by Dr. M— myself. He perceives the world around him as a toy, a game, a device to be manipulated to satisfy his immediate gains.

... I am not a vengeful person, and I do believe that people can change and be rehabilitated – not, however, in the case of Dr. M—.[9]

Dr. S—— M—— M——

TORONTO

Dr. S—— M—— M—— made an application to the College of Physicians and Surgeons of Ontario for reinstatement of his certificate of registration. Dr. M——'s certificate was revoked in 2000 when he admitted to sexual abuse of a patient.

The College did not contest the application, subject to the imposition of specified terms and conditions.

Based on the evidence before the Committee, and all of the circumstances of this case, the Committee concluded that Dr. M—— had satisfied the burden of demonstrating to the satisfaction of the Committee that he could safely be returned to the practice of medicine, subject to the imposition of specified terms, conditions and limitations on his certificate of registration, as proposed by the parties. The Committee concluded that the proposed terms and conditions provide a careful and safe framework for Dr. M——'s re-entry to practice in a supervised manner.

It is notable that the proposed terms, conditions and limitations were largely agreed upon by both the College and Dr. M——. From the Committee's perspective, the terms and conditions provide safeguards to ensure that Dr. M—— is appropriately supported, monitored and assessed in his practice, and treated for his condition. They also provide the Registrar with authority to intervene if any problems arise. The Committee concluded that these terms and conditions were appropriate in all the circumstances.

The Committee therefore directed the Registrar to issue a certificate of registration to the applicant, Dr. M——, subject to the following terms, conditions and limitations:

Dr. M—— will limit his practice to clinical settings that are either team-based or in which other physicians also practice. In non-team based setting, there shall be either a physician or an administrative staff person in the same office setting while Dr. M—— sees patients;

Dr. M—— will cause workplace monitor(s) acceptable to the College, in each setting in which he practices, to execute an undertaking, prior to commencing work in any such setting;

At least once per month, Dr. M—— shall see a psychiatrist who is acceptable to the College, for treatment as required. Dr. M—— shall comply with all treatment recommendations of his psychiatrist;

Dr. M—— shall cause his treating psychiatrist to execute an undertaking, within 30 days of the date of the Order;

If a person who has given an undertaking in the form of a Schedule to the Order is unable or unwilling to continue to fulfill its terms, Dr. M—— shall, within 30 days, obtain an undertaking in the same form from a similarly qualified person who is acceptable to the College;

If any of the reports of the workplace monitor(s) or psychiatrist are not delivered or are unsatisfactory to the College, the Registrar may suspend Dr. M——'s certificate of registration;

Dr. M—— shall undergo and successfully complete to the satisfaction of the College an assessment under the direction of the College in each of his practice settings within 12 months of his return to practice. The assessment will be at Dr. M——'s expense and may include, among other things, an observation component, consultation with his workplace monitor(s) and his treating psychiatrist, and a chart review. Dr. M—— shall comply with any recommendations of the College that result from the assessment;

In the event that Dr. M—— is unsuccessful in the completion of the assessment or in complying with any recommendations that result from the assessment as determined by the College, the Registrar may suspend Dr. M——'s certificate of registration until he successfully completes the assessment or complies with the recommendations;

Dr. M—— shall pay to the College $2,750 to satisfy an outstanding costs order. Such amount shall be paid within six months of the date of this Order; and;

Dr. M—— shall not apply to vary any of the terms of this Order until at least two years have passed from the date of this Order.

SUMMARY

On August 16, 2005, the Discipline Committee ordered the reinstatement of Dr. M—'s certificate of registration, subject to specified terms, conditions and limitations, including that he limit his practice to clinical settings that are either team-based or in which other physicians also practice; there be a workplace monitor acceptable to the College; and he undergo an assessment of his practice within twelve months of returning to practice.

THREE THINGS I'D BE HAPPY TO FORGET

Your dog – Banter? Bunkum? Buckeye?
The cream Lab, nose the size of a baby's
fist and pinker,
tied in the corner closet, seventeen mean feet
from the fireplace, from every dog's birthright.
You shitty bastard.

It's my fault, my fault.

Folly tracks me, wolverines to bleeding hogs.

What you did after your conviction:
bolted to BC, inherited your miser father's island,
took a course, painted Toulouse – forty-seven landscapes
in hues poached from heaven. Met a sweeter boy,
read up on law.

THE COMEBACK KID

Charm, I'll give you that,
and lawyers you keep in meat and candy,
and a voice, *basso Diablo*   that sings
all authorities to snuggles and coos
(I ought to know).

This is what I want to know:
When do my pennies stop dropping
in your best dinner plate? Do you ever toss
coins to beggars and thank me for my taxes, my
nickels and dollars that keep you, plush your pillows,
lacquer your new office, put shoelaces on your brogues,
press your dull shirts, make you respectable again?
Have you ever stopped, once, pen to pad, ready to diagnose,
prescribe, alleviate, impart or shrug
and, calculated, gathered the math ...
He paid for this pen
in chocolate bars, vermouth, that incense
he likes, clotting perfumes.
Richard paid for this, and will again.

Every system protects its earners,
and math is immoral.

Go not in and out of the house of justice,
That thy name may not stink.[10]

It stops here, the chase,
red screeds and blue billets, all audits.

It stops here, the tracing, mincing marionette play
binding effigies for construction-paper pyres.

It stops here, the reprisals and pinching slights,
all this windy rage, fat songs without fades or cold
stops, my shit-cheap *Die Nibelungen*.

Once loved,
better to empty a symbol than sink, sopping
blood-drunk. Better wound down
than winded. It stops here.

NOTES

1. Sameer P. Sarkar, 'Boundary violation and sexual exploitation in psychiatry and psychotherapy: a review,' *Advances in Psychiatric Treatment*, July 2004, 313.

2. M. Cohen and others, 'Sanctions against sexual abuse of patients by doctors: sex difference in attitudes among young family physicians,' *Canadian Medical Association Journal*, July 1995, http://www.cmaj.ca/cgi/content/abstract/153/2/169.

3. Pierre Assalian and Marc Ravart, 'Management of professional sexual misconduct: Evaluation and recommendations,' *Journal of Sexual and Reproductive Medicine*, Autumn 2003, 91-92.

4. Ibid, 89.

5. *A Gun Makes an Awful Mess*, VHS, directed by RM Vaughan and Michael Achtman (Toronto: Vtape, 1998).

6. *Mr. Danvers*, VHS, directed by RM Vaughan and Michael Achtman (Toronto: Vtape, 2000).

7. *Rx*, VHS, directed by RM Vaughan and Laura Cowell (Toronto: Canadian Filmmakers Distribution Centre, 2001).

8. Francoise Sagan, *Lost Profile*, trans. Joanna Kilmartin (New York: Penguin, 1978), 132.

9. RM Vaughan, letter to Counsel, College of Physicians and Surgeons of Ontario, July 20, 2005.

10. *The Wisdom of Anii* (900 BCE).

AUTHOR'S NOTE

'Based on a true story' is putting it lightly.

The events described in this poetic memoir happened to me, and I have attempted to recount them with as much veracity, unpleasant as it sometimes is for all concerned, as possible. All documents reproduced are true copies of actual correspondence.

I have written this book for many reasons, but chief among them is the hope that in some small way it will help to prevent such abuses from happening again and/or to offer those who have been similarly abused at least a partial (and admittedly imperfect) mirror.

Odd as it may sound, given all my rage, I consider this book an act of forgiveness.

ACKNOWLEDGEMENTS

Ten thousand thanks to Kevin Connolly for shepherding me through this often difficult book and for putting up with my ten thousand neuroses.

Thanks also to Alana Wilcox for her sharp-minded editing, and the cookies. I also owe a great debt of gratitude to Michael Holmes, my dear friend and best advice-giver, who encouraged me to write this book in the first place. Finally, thanks to my friends and fellow writers Jared Mitchell, Nathanaël Stephens and Warren Dunford, who heard early versions of this book and, against all odds and common sense, told me to carry on.

Earlier versions of poems contained in this collection appeared in *Taddle Creek*, *This Magazine* and *The Fiddlehead*.

ABOUT THE AUTHOR

RM Vaughan is a Toronto-based writer and video artist originally from New Brunswick. His books include the poetry collections *A Selection of Dazzling Scarves*, *Invisible to Predators* and *Ruined Stars*, the novels *A Quilted Heart* and *Spells*, and the plays *Camera, Woman* and *The Monster Trilogy*. Vaughan's poems, essays, plays and fiction appear in over forty national and international anthologies. Vaughan's short video and film works are exhibited in festivals and galleries across Canada and around the world. Vaughan comments on art and culture for numerous publications and is a two-time National Magazine Award nominee.

Please visit www.rmvaughan.ca.

Typeset in Bulmer
Printed and bound at the Coach House on bpNichol Lane, 2008

Edited for the press by Kevin Connolly
Designed by Evan Munday
Cover by Evan Munday
Author photo by Jared Mitchell

Coach House Books
401 Huron Street on bpNichol Lane
Toronto Ontario M5S 2G5

416 979 2217
800 367 6360

mail@chbooks.com
www.chbooks.com